Mayan Astronomy: The History of the Maya's Measurements of the Planets and Stars

By Charles River Editors

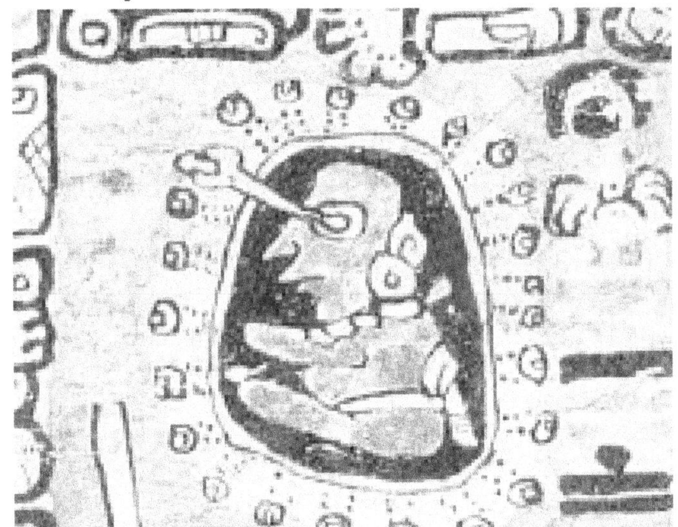

An illustration in the *Madrid Codex* believed to depict an astronomer

About Charles River Editors

Charles River Editors was founded by Harvard and MIT alumni to provide superior editing and original writing services, with the expertise to create digital content for publishers across a vast range of subject matter. In addition to providing original digital content for third party publishers, Charles River Editors republishes civilization's greatest literary works, bringing them to a new generation via ebooks.

Sign up here to receive updates about free books as we publish them, and visit Our Kindle Author Page to browse today's free promotions and our most recently published Kindle titles.

Introduction

A picture of the Caracol at Chichen Itza, which is believed to have been an observatory

Many ancient civilizations have influenced and inspired people in the 21st century, and the Greeks and Romans continue to fascinate the West today, but of all the world's civilizations, none have intrigued people more than the Mayans, whose culture, astronomy, language, and mysterious disappearance all continue to captivate people. In the past decade especially, there has been a renewed focus on the Mayans, whose advanced calendar led many to speculate the world would end on the same date the Mayan calendar ended in 2012.

The focus on the "doomsday" scenario, however, overshadowed the Mayans' true contributions to astronomy, language, sports, and art. While many incorrectly presume that the Maya were predicting the world to end on that date, it is not a coincidence that their calendar ended on the winter solstice. The Maya developed a sophisticated method of calculating and creating a calendar that is astonishing even by today's standards, and their advancements in applied mathematics not only has intrigued archaeologists but has been incorporated into the beliefs of New Agers and modern apocalyptic doomsayers. In the history of arithmetic, their use of zero stands as a milestone of great significance, which placed them ahead of contemporary Europeans. In Europe, this essential concept was not part of the canon of calculation until the Renaissance.

For the Maya, astronomy was not a purely scientific pursuit but intimately linked to religious, mythological, and ideological elements that were of the highest importance. The celestial realm held a sacred nature, as did the many gods and goddesses that dwelt there, so for all Mesoamerican cultures, astronomy was a fundamental part of their everyday lives. Thus, astronomy was present in their calendars, religion, and even agriculture, and in close relation to astronomy, the concept of time was also an essential part of their worldview. The Maya recorded time on almost every surface they could, including lintels, cornices, panels, stelae, friezes, ceramics, and paper. This insistence on capturing dates has led many scholars to suggest the Maya were obsessed with time.

The Maya had some of the most advanced astronomical measurements in the world, and their work built upon thousands of years, spanning from around 2500 BCE until the the arrival of the Spanish in 1519.[1] Thanks to their hieroglyphic writing, archaeologists have been able to learn a wealth of information about the way they lived and their complex system of beliefs. Susan Milbrath, a leading expert on Mayan astronomy, noted that the "study of Pre-Columbian Maya astronomical imagery must begin with an understanding of the contemporary Maya worldview, because we cannot hope to penetrate the ancient beliefs without an understanding of what the Maya say about the heavens today."[2] Many contemporary Mayans still use one or several of the ancient calendars, as well as Precolumbian rituals and astronomical cycles.[3]

Mayan Astronomy: The History of the Maya's Measurements of the Planets and Stars examines what is known and unknown about the Maya's astronomy, and why their astronomy was among the most accurate in the world. Along with pictures and a bibliography for further reading,

---

[1] Metcalfe, 2020

[2] Milbrath, 1999, p. 12

[3] For detailed information see Milbrath (1999, ch. 1).

you will learn about Mayan astronomy like never before.

The Enigma of the Maya

Depiction of Upakal K'inich in Palenque

Ubiquitous in popular and scholarly descriptions of Maya civilization is the word enigma. In spite of tremendous advances in archaeology that continue to reveal more and more information on the highly developed Maya civilization of Mesoamerica, there remain many unanswered questions. Two examples of significant unresolved questions concerning the Maya illustrate the serious holes in our knowledge. Despite the existence of their civilization in

South America for thousands of years, historians and archaeologists still cannot explain where the Maya came from or exactly why their civilization collapsed.

Why have these questions continued to go unanswered? These unsolved mysteries surrounding the Maya civilization persist in large measure due to the efficiency of the Spanish in eradicating the remnants of Maya culture. And unlike the Aztecs, the disappearance of the Mayans cannot be clearly traced to a series of battles. By the early 16th century, the Spanish conquistadors, along with the colonists and zealous propagators of the faith who followed the likes of Cortes and Pizarro, set out to systematically destroy the indigenous Maya civilization of the Yucatan that was already in decline even before their arrival. The land-grabbing colonists used the natives as virtual slave labor and pillaged their cities, while enthusiastic Catholic baptizers did their best to erase their heathen beliefs.

While the blame for the loss of much of the Mayan culture can be heaped upon the Spanish, much of what is known about life in a Maya community came from the writings of the Provincial of the Franciscans in the Yucatan, Bishop Diego de Landa. His 1566 book, *Relación de las cosas de Yucatán* (*An Account of the Affairs in the Yucatan*), contains detailed observations on the culture of the Maya, including a record of their hieroglyphics and writing system. These have proved to be invaluable sources for those piecing together a picture of Mayan life. But Bishop Landa was also responsible for what in retrospect was an incalculable loss for the world. The Mayans developed the only full language during the Mesoamerican period, but Landa and his Franciscan cohorts confiscated a great number of books written in the Mayan language which they believed were full of heretical ideas and burned them all. Bishop Landa's well-intentioned bonfire of books left the world with only four extant Maya manuscripts and a 1558 record written in Latin characters of Maya cosmology called the *Popol Vuh*, or book of the people preserving oral tradition of the K'iche Maya of Guatemala.

The Maya's writings obviously weren't the only things lost to history. In the years after the conquest of the Maya some of their cities were mined by the colonists for building materials. A spectacular example of this is took place at Izamal, where Bishop Landa's Monastery of San Antonio de Padua was constructed with stones reused from a Maya building. The Monastery itself, rising above the colonial town, sits on a plinth that is, in fact, a truncated Maya pyramid. Other Maya cities still inhabited in the period of conquest were abandoned and eventually obscured by jungle vegetation. Explorers in the jungle still find lost ruins of the Maya in Central America, and one incorrect story that made the rounds in 2011 speculated that Mayan ruins were found in North Georgia, a reflection of the interest and uncertainty still surrounding the Maya.

In the early 19th century, explorers and adventurers began to rediscover several Maya sites. Following the opinions of the colonists. who at the time perceived the contemporary Maya as unsophisticated and culturally impoverished, the explorers were initially convinced that these people could not have been responsible for such elaborate building projects. Given some of their similarities to the ancient civilizations in Europe and Egypt, they concluded that the Maya pyramids and other structures they discovered must have somehow been the work of Greeks, Romans, Egyptians or Indians from India. How exactly these American city builders got to the region was explained by fanciful conjecture on cultural migration.

In the middle of the 19th century, John Lloyd Stephens and the topographical artist Frederick Catherwood systematically explored the Mayan ruins of British Honduras, Guatemala and the Yucatan. The subsequent publication of Stephens' description of the Maya ruins and Catherwood's illustrations in *Incidents of Travel in Central America, Chiapas, and the Yucatán* in 1841 and *Incidents of Travel in Yucatán* in 1843 were best sellers. They were also responsible for an upsurge in interest in the mysteries of lost civilizations. In the last half of the 19th century, a number of other explorers recorded Maya sites, and in 1881, English archaeologist Alfred Maudslay began the first modern scientific study of a number of Maya cities. His work inspired American archaeologists associated with Harvard University to undertake expeditions, and these in turn were followed by many university and museum sponsored digs right up to the present day. Interest in the Maya began an upswing that carries through today.

The many (and ongoing) accounts of discoveries of Mayan cities by archaeologists and explorers have only added to the mysteries of the Maya civilization, which in turn continue to fuel interest and speculation. Early archaeologists attributed names to the buildings in many sites based on assumptions as to their use, which has led to misleading descriptions that should be paid little attention. At Uxmal, today a very popular Yucatan tourist destination, there are buildings called the Nunnery and the Governor's Palace, both of which are based on quite fanciful ideas of the original purpose of the structures. At Chichén Itzá, the greatest Maya city in the Yucatan, one is taken by guides to a building called the Nunnery for no good reason other than the small rooms reminded the Spaniards of a nunnery back home. Similarly the great pyramid at Chichén Itzá is designated the El Castillo, the Castle, which it certainly is not, and the Observatory is called El Caracol, the Snail, for its spiral staircase. This kind of confusing naming of Maya structures had been abandoned at recently discovered sites and replaced with less colorful terms such as, for example,

Temple 1, Temple II and so on at Tikal in Guatemala.

The Pyramid of the Magician at Uxmal and Building of the Iguana at Uxmal

The Castle at Chichén Itzá

Today the Aztecs are remembered as the civilization with the vast South American empire, but the Mayans spread across a wide swath of land themselves. The region of Mesoamerica inhabited by the Maya stretched from the dry, flat limestone plains of the Yucatan to the wet, mountainous jungle of Chiapas and Guatemala and on to the narrow flatland of the Pacific coast. The first inhabitants of the region are believed to have been hunter gatherers, and anthropologists think these primitive people were descended from the early migrants who moved from Asia across to the northern reaches of North America and spread south around 14000 BCE. Once settled, a more agricultural society developed in central Mexico in the fifth millennium BCE.

These people were able to reliably grow crops of corn, beans and squashes through slash and burn field preparation, but depending on the quantity and quality of the soil, a field had a limited life expectancy. In some regions, particularly those where the soil cover was thin and the rainfall limited, the slash and burn technique of crop cultivation required careful attention to the seasonal weather pattern.

Around 1800 BCE, the Olmecs, the earliest traceable civilization of Mesoamerica, built cities that depended on reliable agricultural production. Many details of Olmec society remain a mystery, but it is known that some of their practices, such as building pyramids and playing a ritual ball-game, were similar to those of the later Maya. Nevertheless, the precise relationship between the Olmec and the Maya culture is as yet unknown. What is known is that while the earliest Maya communities on the Pacific coast and in the Guatemalan highlands and Belize were on the rise, the Olmec civilization, with its population centers near the region of modern Veracruz and Villahermosa in Mexico, was in decline.

The history of the Maya is divided into periods that have been given names and dates that are not currently unanimously accepted. The nomenclature of the chronology of Maya civilization was created by Eurocentric scholars who held fixed ideas on the rise, flourishing and decline of civilizations, in keeping with the tracking of the Greek and

Roman empires of antiquity. In particular, readers should be cautious of the word classic, as it implies a superior rank or model or standard which does not really apply to the evolution of Maya culture. Still, this chronology, even with its imperfections, does allow for a quick survey of the evolution of Maya civilization.

The Early Preclassic period dating from 1800-900 BCE is the era when the Olmecs established their major cities at Paso de la Amada in Chiapas and San Lorenzo in southern Veracruz. In the Middle Preclassic Period, spanning the years from 900-300 BCE, the first Maya cities were built on the Pacific coast, in places like Itzapa near Tapachula, in the Guatemalan highlands at such sites as Kaminaljuyú now underneath Guatemala City, and the recently excavated mega-city El Mirador. It is currently held that Maya city building expanded north further into the Guatemalan Highlands and Belize.

Pyramid at El Mirador

It was in the Late Preclassic Period from 300 BCE – 250 CE that archaeologists believe Maya culture developed a high level of complexity. This included the appearance of writing in the Mayan language and a sophisticated continuing calendar system. In the Early Classic Period, 250-600, Maya civilization flourished, particularly in the city of Tikal in modern Guatemala. Major construction was carried out at Copán in modern Honduras and at Palenque in Chiapas, Mexico. The Late Classic period, 600-950, is used by Mayanists to designate the age in which civilization reached its height. This was the time when the great cities of the Yucatan or northern lowlands flourished and the cities of the southern lowlands declined. It was also late in this period that the city of Chichén Itzá rose to prominence.

The Main Plaza at Tikal

   The final period in the chronology used by scholars of Maya civilization is the Post Classic Period, which spanned from 950-1530 and saw saw the collapse of Chichén Itzá and the rise of Mayapán, the last leading city of Maya culture. The four surviving Mayan codices were written during this period.

   Given the manner in which Maya cities flourished in different periods and were built in different environments, from the lush jungle in the south to the wet coastlands of Belize and the dry limestone plains of the Yucatan, it is not surprising that the Maya were not a homogenous group. In different regions of their empire, Mayan people and cities had distinctly different economies, social organization, art, and architecture. Variation existed over time and geography, which is important to keep that in mind when discussing Mayan culture and history.

The Mayan Calendar

The Mayan calendar is known for its accuracy[4] and has both ceremonial and practical functions, but what people today commonly call the Mayan calendar is actually a system of several calendars corresponding to solar, lunar, and planetary cycles. The three main calendars are the *Haab*, which is the 365-day solar calendar, the *Tzolkin*, which is the 260-day ceremonial calendar, and the Calendar Round, which is a 52-day cycle. The Maya also created the Long Count, used to record events chronologically.

Despite the fact that it shares some elements with other Mesoamerican calendars, the Mayan calendar is a unique development that directly corresponds to their particular worldview. Most scholars agree that the 260-day calendar originated in the Olmec area around 900-700 BCE and spread from there to the rest of Mesoamerica.[5] Linguistic evidence suggests the *Tzolkin* calendar was probably adopted by the Maya around 600 BCE, whereas the earliest evidence of the *Haab* is from 300 BCE, and the Long Count seems to date back to around 250 BCE. There are some who believe their origins could go back as far as 2000 BCE, but there is insufficient data to support these claims.[6]

The existing knowledge of the calendars' structure and

---

[4] "The Mayan Prediction," 2012
[5] See Milbrath (2017).
[6] Milbrath, 2017

contents comes from four types of sources: original Mayan inscriptions found on pottery and stone; ancient codices; colonial documents; and ethnographic descriptions passed down through the oral tradition.

The *Haab* is a solar calendar composed of 365 days. The year is divided into 18 *uinals,* or months, of 20 days each and a final month of five days, called *Wayeb.* Each *uinal* has its own name and glyph. During Wayeb, ceremonies and celebrations were held to mark the closing of a cycle and the beginning of a new one.

Spanish chronicler Diego de Landa wrote the following in relation to the Maya's 365-day calendar: "With the letters of these Indians, which I have given above in Chapter CX, they gave names to [the days of] their months, and with all the months joined together they made a sort of calendar, by the aid of which they regulated not only their festivals but also their accounts, contracts and businesses as we do with ours… For, although the characters and the days of their months are twenty, they have the habit of counting them from one to thirteen; after these thirteen, they turn back and begin with one, and they thus divide the days of the year into twenty-seven thirteenths and nine days, without counting the unlucky days."[7]

In addition to the solar calendar, the Maya had a

---

[7] Tozzer, 1941, p. 148

ceremonial calendar called *Tzolkin*. This calendar is not divided into months but is instead made up of 20 named days that combine with 13 numbers to give a total of 260 days. Any combination of named day and number only appears once in the 260-day cycle. In the *Tzolkin*, years always began on one of four days, called "year bearers."

The calendar corresponds to nine Moon cycles and coincides with the human gestational period. It was used to predict a person's destiny based on their date of birth and determine the best times to plant crops. The *Tzolkin* also corresponded to the cycle of the planet Venus.

It is possible that the *Tzolkin* developed from a natural subdivision of the *Haab* in relation to the agricultural year, which lasts 260 days. This agricultural cycle is still in use by many modern Mayan farmers. In fact, some of these groups still divide the maize cycle into 13 sections of 20 days each.

A complete date for the Maya consists of the combination of a *Haab* and a *Tzolkin* date, and the interweaving of both calendars makes up what archaeologists call the Calendar Round. Each combination of a *Haab* and *Tzolkin* date occurs only once every 52 years, and this period is considered a complete cycle. The importance of the 52-year cycle extended past its calendrical significance - the Maya believed that any person reaching 52 years of age held special wisdom and was respected as an elder. The last

Calendar Round was completed on April 28, 2011, and the next one will be completed on April 5, 2063.

The Long Count is the Maya's continuous record of time in chronological order. This calendar works in combination with the *Haab* and *Tzolkin* to place events, both historical and mythological, within a 5,125-year span. It functions similar to the Gregorian calendar, using days, months, years, centuries, and even millennia to track the passage of time and pinpoint events along a timeline.

The basic unit of the Long Count is the *kin* or day, and from there, a series of units of time are used to represent different lengths of time. The following chart shows these units of time and their equivalents:

Unit of time	Equal to
kin	1 day
uinal	20 kins (20 days)
tun	18 uninals (360 days)

katun   20 tuns (7,200 days)

baktun   20 katuns (144,000 days)

After much debate, the most widely accepted date for the beginning of the Long Count is August 13th, 3114 BCE,[8] which corresponds to the Mayan date of 13.0.0.0.0 4 *Ajaw* 8 *Kumk'u*.[9] This was a mythological date in which the Sun was at its zenith at noon, and the Turtle constellation (Orion) marked the underworld.

Dates were typically written in paired vertical columns, with the *baktuns* occupying the highest position. A full cycle is made up of 13 baktuns, which meant that the next time the date would be 13.0.0.0.0 is December 21st, 2012. This date simply meant the end of a Long Count cycle; however, misinterpretations associated it with "a prophecy of the end of the world."[10]

---

[8] See Casares Contreras (2016, pp. 19-20).

[9] 13 baktun, 0 katun, 0 tun, 0 uinal, 0 kin = 13.0.0.0.0. 4 Ajaw 8 Kumk'u corresponds to the date on the Calendar Round.

[10] Hocken and Kher, 2021

Jan Pesula's picture of a stela at Quiriguá with a Long Count date

The Mayan system for recording time can be described by a series of basic characteristics. First, there is the use of different calendars for short, medium, and long periods, and then there is the use of different cycles. All of this is combined in their integration of cyclical and linear time.

All Mayan dates begin from the mythical date of 13.0.0.0.0 4 *Ajaw* 8 *Kumk'u* (August 13, 3114 BCE) and record time passed from that point to the date they measure. The last date recorded on a public monument using the Long Count was found in Tonina, Chiapas, and it marked the date 10.4.0.0.0 12 *Ahaw* 3 *Wo* (January 15, 909 CE). During the late Classic period, the Maya stopped inscribing Long Count dates on public monuments and began using abbreviated systems for recording time instead. The fact that no later dates were recorded does not, however, mean that the Long Count was no longer used; it simply means that they stopped including this information on public monuments. Many examples of Long Count dates after that time still appear in codices.

When the first Spanish conquistadores arrived in the Yucatan Peninsula, they noticed that the Maya counted time using lunar phases. Chronicler Diego de Landa wrote, "They have their perfect year like ours, of 365 days and 6 hours. They divide it in two kinds of months, the first one of 30 days that is called *u'*, which means Moon, and they counted it since it came out until it ceased to show. The other kind of month had 20 days, and it was called *winal jun ek' eh*."[11] According to de Landa, the Maya had two ways of counting time, one based on the yearly solar calendar and a second one based on the lunar cycle. The Maya seem to have

---

[11] Diego de Landa cited in Iwaniszewski (2012).

incorporated the counting of lunar cycles into the Long Count, which were recorded with a set of six glyphs called lunar series. This series was used to express exactly in which part of the cycle a given date fell.[12]

It is important to note that the Mayan language does not have specific verb tenses to indicate when an action took place, so an additional mechanism was needed to portray time in monumental inscriptions. This is where the Long Count came into play, and it also explains why the Maya were seemingly so obsessed with recording the date of everything. J.H. Linden explained, "Almost all Maya inscriptions begin with a date. On Classic period monuments these dates are usually recorded in a sequence of glyphs called the Initial Series. Each Initial Series glyph designates the position of the recorded date in various chronological and calendric systems of the Classic period Maya. The normal reading order for Maya hieroglyphs is from top to bottom, left to right, in horizontal pairs."[13]

Each Initial Series consists of nine glyphs, the first five corresponding to the Long Count date and the following four glyphs including the *Haab* and *Tzolkin* plus two additional glyphs, marking the position of the Long Count date in various calendric cycles. The Lunar Series is a set of five glyphs that follows the Initial Series. These glyphs were

---

[12] See Iwaniszewski (2012).
[13] Linden, 1986, p. 122

used by the Maya to record the lunar synodic calendar. The first one records the day position of the Long Count date in the current lunar month. The second one records the position of that month in the current six-month lunar semester. The next glyph records the position in an 18-month lunar calendar. The final glyph specifies if the current lunar month has 29 or 30 days.

A basic component of Mayan astronomy and their calendar system was mathematics, used in many aspects of daily life but also to predict astronomical phenomena and make rather sophisticated calendrical calculations. The Mayan mathematical system is vigesimal, which means that the base number used for making calculations is 20 instead of 10, which many modern socictics arc uscd to today. Thc Maya's system of calculations uses a dot to represent the number one, a stick to represent the number five, and a shell to represent the number 0. Combining these signs, they were able to write very large numbers and carry out a variety of complex mathematical operations.

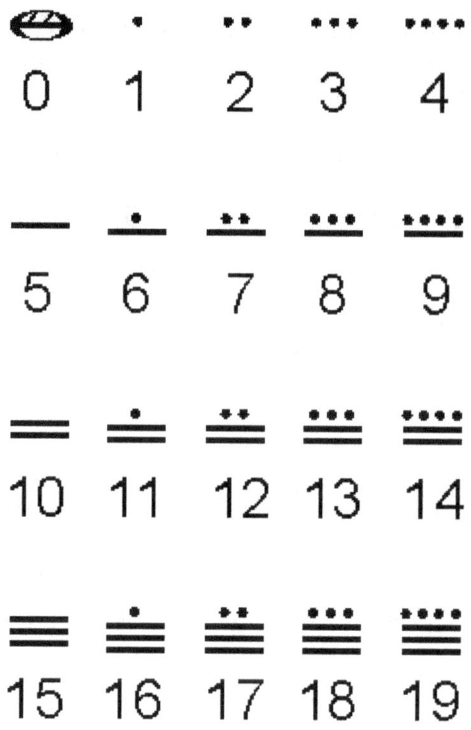

0	1	2	3	4
5	6	7	8	9
10	11	12	13	14
15	16	17	18	19

Mayan numerology

A noteworthy aspect of the Mayan representations of time is that they portrayed units of time as animate objects. All units were represented in three ways: symbolic or geometrical, by a head variant or personified, and by a full figure. Numbers, in their simplest form, were represented by the bar-dot system, but they could also be represented by head variants - the heads of the gods of each number - which could be anthropomorphic or zoomorphic.[14] All animals used to represent units of time were associated with rain and water and were thus representations of fertility. Rivera Valencia explained, "Some represent the water currents generated by downpours, others announce the arrival of the

---

[14] See Rice (2008, pp. 286-288).

storms, or are associated with the winds that bring them. This relationship lets us infer that, in the Maya area, the calendric year was fixed in association to the rainy season and not to the solar transit. This hypothesis clarifies the origin of the word, haab', 'year,' which even nowadays has the meaning of 'rain,' or 'storm' in some Mayan languages."[15]

Unit of time	Zoomorphic representation	Symbolic representation
Kin	Monkey	Four-petaled flower
Uninal	Frog or toad	Moon
Tun	Watersnake or mythological bird	Drum
Katun	Mythological bird	Tun sign combined with Kawak[16]
Baktun	Mythological bird	Two Kawak glyphs

---

[15] Valencia, 2017, p. 399

[16] Kawak is a day sign that is used to represent "count."

In the *Relacion de las cosas de Yucatan*, Landa dedicates a lot of time to find a correlation between the Mayan and Christian calendars. As a priest, he was greatly familiar with the complexities of the religious calendar, and he used his knowledge of the subject to attempt to understand the workings of the different Mayan calendars. Even though he considered them to be the work of the devil, Landa's admiration for the intricate time-keeping devices of the Yucatan natives is evident. His detailed observations came up with the following correlation:[17]

Christian Date	Maya Date	Event
January 15th	12 Ben 10 Ch'en	Beginning of Christian year
July 15th	12 Lamat 5 Uayeb	End of Maya year
July 16th	12 Kan 1 Pop	Beginning of Maya year
December 31st	11 Eb 9 Ch'en	End of Christian Year

Tozzer noted, "The first day of the year with these people

was always on the sixteenth day of our month of July, and the first of their month of Pop. And there is no reason to be astonished that th[ese] people, although simple as we have found them in other things, should also have shown an interest in this, and should have a knowledge of it like that possessed by other nations."[18]

The Mayan Concept of Time

The ancient Maya developed a unique concept of time that combines modern society's traditional idea of linear time with the notion of cyclical time. "Time is a form of social knowledge inherent to each culture,"[19] and this fact is more than evident in the case of the Maya.

The Maya's interest in time was multi-dimensional - they were concerned with the succession of seasonal cycles, atmospheric phenomena, and astral movements because the information they gathered was used to regulate a variety of activities, from agriculture and hunting to social events and mythical occurrences. In the world of the ancient Maya, time existed in unison with the movement of the Sun and the Moon, expressing itself in its most basic form through the cycles of the human body. Day and night, wakefulness and sleep all obeyed this rotation linked to their dual way of measuring time, on a cosmic scale and on a human one. As de Orellana put it, "Undisputed lord and master of time,

---

[18] Tozzer, 1941, p. 150
[19] De Orellana et al., 2012, p. 84

Maya civilization was at the same time its worshipper and its vassal, as it was ruled over by a multitude of deities who governed the days, the months, the years, the katuns…and even the numbers that preceded each of those periods of time to better situate them in calendars."[20]

A society's view on the past often depends on the way they perceive time and its movement. Traditionally, time is thought of as being linear or cyclical. Linear time follows a sequence of events, while cyclical time implies the repetition of events in a perpetual loop. For the Maya, these two concepts of time coexisted, and linear time was incorporated into a cyclical pattern. This combination of linear and cyclical time became the foundation of their entire worldview, and it governed every aspect of their lives. "Time itself was the sacred ruler; humans were merely its mortal and temporal custodians."[21]

For the Maya, time and calendars were crucial instruments for understanding the past, but more importantly, they were key elements for constructing their future. In contrast, history was "the result of a dialectic between the past and the present…Current happenings were interpreted to fit patterns established by the past, and the past was reconceived to accommodate present circumstances."[22] Yet, there is still another interesting way in which the Maya perceived time—

---

[20] De Orellana et al., 2012, p. 82
[21] Rice (2007) cited in Rice (2008, p. 294).
[22] Umberger (1987) cited in Rice (2008, p. 294).

mythical time is different from ordinary time, and in it, the past, present, and future coexist and beings can exist and move freely through these different temporal realms. "Time is cosmic order, its cyclical patterning the counterforce to the randomness of evil."[23]

While linear-time was closely linked to political power, genealogies of ruling dynasties and the recording of important actions in the lives of their rulers, cyclical time was associated with prophecies, allowing the Maya to anticipate events and carry out rituals to make unfavourable periods on the calendar more auspicious. There were three kinds of omens: predictions of days, yearly prophecies (also called tunic prophesies after the unit of time, *tun*), and *katunic* prophesies. These last prophecies were presented on a *katun* wheel, which consists of a sequence of 13 periods of 20 years that repeats in a cyclical pattern. One cycle corresponds to 260 years. Among the prophetic elements contained in the katun cycle were conquests, migrations, the falling of cities, and political treason, to name a few.

The Maya's knowledge of time gave the impression of predictability, and astronomer priests seemed to have full control over astronomical phenomena through the use of ceremonies and rituals. J.J. Mark explained, "Forward astronomical predictions were based upon careful observations of the skies but were understood according to

---

[23] Farriss, 1987, p. 574

the belief system which governed their understanding of how the universe worked and that understanding was that time was cyclical, not linear."[24] Inevitably, there were unpredictable events, so the Mayan priests explained them away as being accidental but also a part of the larger plan all along. This allowed these priests to wield an enormous amount of power in Mayan society.

For the Precolumbian Maya, time seemed to be an integral part of their political and religious ideology, and for the ruling class, time was also synonymous with power. The development of their calendars became a highly effective system for exercising that power, giving rulers a means of imposing social, political, and religious control. Later on, during the colonial period, the Maya's notion of time, still based on the *Haab* and *Tzolkin*, became mixed with elements from the Julian calendar and the Christian *Book of Saints*. The *Chilam Balam* is a perfect example of this syncretism.

In Mayan representations, time was displayed as an animate being, and calendrical elements were conceived as anthropomorphic deities that carried the units of time along a cosmic journey. Day names were inspired by natural phenomena such as rain, storms, grass, earth, wind, death, the Moon, and the names of animals. The names for periods of time animated the representations of these day-names and

---

[24] Mark, 2012

personified them so that keeping records of time became almost like telling a story.[25]

In addition to recording time and astronomical events, calendars are also a very important part of social life. "Time is a social construct [and it] becomes socially 'real' in relation to recurrent ritual activities."[26] In this sense, a calendar integrates the way in which a society views time, through concepts like reckoning and duration, in the form of a systematic tool. P.M. Rice explained, "Although we cannot study time-consciousness and duration directly among ancient individuals or societies, we can examine how time is *represented*."[27] "Time-reckoning" is an important part of this representation, and it includes the different ways of telling time through the coordination of a particular event with certain reference points, such as astronomical, meteorological, or cultural phenomena. Calendars are thus used to record continuous time-reckoning.

Precolumbian Astronomy

In addition to being a fundamental part of the different calendars, astronomy was also present in mythology, religious rituals, military campaigns, ceremonies of legitimacy, agriculture, and city planning. "The Maya recognized that the natural world, the cosmos, and even their

[25] Rice, 2008, p. 291
[26] Rice, 2008, p. 276
[27] Rice, 2008, p. 277

own bodies functioned according to observable cycles. To locate themselves within these cycles they tracked the movement of planets, the Moon, and the Sun."[28]

The Sun and Moon, the planets, and astronomical events like eclipses, solstices, and equinoxes were all associated with important parts of the Mayan worldview and formed a part of the planning and organization of all kinds of events and activities. For example, the Maya believed that eclipses happened when the Sun was possessed by a monster and attempted to devour the Moon. Beliefs of this kind marked the need for specific rituals and ceremonies to maintain the balance of the cosmos. "It is necessary to emphasize…that every astronomical mechanism, just like everything else in Maya[n] life, had to be related to the 260-day sacred almanac [sic]."[29]

In the Post-Classic and colonial periods, political and religious officials of noble birth were required to train as Sun-priests, called *aj k'in*. Important Mayan cities had specialized "astronomer priests"[30] that seemed to control the movements of the stars and planets and make astronomical events happen. This was used to legitimize power by matching the dates of important events with specific celestial phenomena: "While there is no doubt that the commoners

---

[28] Zorich, 2012, p. 25

[29] Thompson, 1974, p. 86

[30] The term "astronomer priest" was coined by John Eric Sydney Thompson. See Casares Contreras (2016, pp. 69-70).

were familiar with many aspects of the calendrical
system…the ability to determine critical dates and to lay out
accurate alignments to the corresponding solar events was
obviously not a public domain based on a commonly shared
world view, but rather part of the esoteric knowledge
reserved for the elite."[31]

Even though the majority of the population did not have
access to specialized astronomical knowledge, it was still a
key component of many of their activities. They all used
astronomy to a greater or lesser degree throughout their daily
lives, whether it was to plan the next agricultural cycle or
determine if their child's date of birth was auspicious or not.

The Sun was the most important element and played a vital
role in many aspects of Mayan life. In politics, for example,
rulers or ruling dynasties were often associated with it, so it
was linked to power. In addition, Kinich Ahau, the Sun god,
was one of the most important deities in the Mayan
pantheon. There are many representations of the Sun
throughout Mayan art, including many of its different
attributes related to plants and animals. For example, in
certain contexts, the Sun could be represented as a flower, a
jaguar, a scarlet macaw, or a monkey.

One of the main uses of the solar calendar was in
agriculture. The ancient Mayan diet was based on corn, and

---

[31] Milbrath, 1999, p. 208

the clearing of fields, the planting of seeds, and the harvest all corresponded to seasonal cycles. Sowing and harvesting were often aligned with the two yearly solar zeniths. The *Tzolkin* was also used to determine the most auspicious days for some agricultural activities. Additionally, colonial records state that the Mayan festival calendar was organized according to the solar seasons.[32]

Most Mayan codices or written manuscripts were burned by Franciscan missionaries in the 16th century, but three undisputed texts were preserved: *The Dresden Codex*, *The Madrid Codex*, and *The Paris Codex*. The authenticity of a fourth document, *The Grolier Codex*, is still under debate. The contents of these documents include historical accounts, rituals, and astronomical data, the latter being presented in the form of tables or almanacs. Vail and Aveni wrote that the "two [were] distinguished by whether they include dates in the absolute [Long Count] calendar used by the Maya [tables] or are organized in terms of the 260-day ritual calendar used throughout Mesoamerica for divination and prophecy [almanacs]."[33] The almanacs of the three accepted codices contain tables tracking the movements of planets, solar and lunar eclipses, solstices and equinoxes, and other seasonal celestial phenomena, but, they do not contain Long Count dates.

---

[32] Documents like the *Chilam Balam* written in 1758 and Diego de Landa's 16th century texts narrate different events that correspond to the solar cycle.

[33] Vail and Aveni, 2004, p. 5

The Dresden Codex is one of the four surviving Mayan
pictorial manuscripts that date back to the 13th century.
Drawn on a 358-centimeter piece of *amate*[34] paper, the
codex contains 39 leaves with writing on both sides and has
an accordion format. This document has been extremely
valuable for the study of Mayan astronomy since it "depicts
hieroglyphs and numerals and figures, and contains ritual
and divination calendars, calculations of the phases of
Venus, eclipses of the Sun and Moon, instructions relating to
new-year ceremonies, and descriptions of the locations of
the Rain God, which culminate in a full-page miniature
showing a great deluge."[35]

Studies conducted by Ernst Förstermann in the 19th century
found that information concerning numbers, day names,
deities, and astronomical events in *The Dresden Codex*
corresponded to the 260-day calendar. The data retrieved
also helped expand the understanding of the Long Count.
There are 27 Long Count dates found in the codex, and a
series of Calendar Round dates, corresponding to the period
between 1100 and 1250, including dates accurately
recording events related to Venus.

The Madrid Codex has 56 leaves painted on both sides,
making it the longest of the surviving codices. Dating back
to the 13th or 14th century, it is also made from *amate* paper

---

[34] Amate is a type of bark paper widely used throughout Mesoamerica.
[35] "The Dresden Codex," 2017

and folded in an accordion format. It contains 250 almanacs that cover a diversity of subjects, such as "rain ceremonies associated with the deity Chaak, agricultural activities, ceremonies to commemorate the end of one year and the start of the next, deer hunting and trapping, the sacrifice of captives and other events associated with the five nameless days [Wayeb] at the end of the year, carving deity images, and beekeeping."[36] There are no Long Count dates in *The Madrid Codex*, but it does include a wide variety of astronomical information in its almanacs.

The Paris Codex is thought to have been made between the 13th and 15th centuries and is the most damaged of the surviving manuscripts. It focuses mainly on Mayan rituals and ceremonies. Drawn on amate and folded in accordion style, the document has 11 leaves containing columns of glyphs and images on both sides. Some of these leaves contain images of animals that appear to be associated with a set of 13 constellations. This has led some researchers to believe this corresponds to a zodiac.[37]

The Chilam Balam is a collection of books believed to have been written by a prophet. The word *balam* means jaguar, and these are said to be the books of the Prophet Jaguar. These books appeared in colonial times, written in the Mayan language but using the European alphabet, and began

---

[36] Vail and Aveni, 2004, p. 5
[37] Vail and Aveni, 2004, p. 5

to circulate throughout the Yucatan Peninsula. The books contain traditional Mayan cosmology combined with elements of Catholicism.

The contents of *The Chilam Balam* are vast, including things like almanacs, prophesies, maps, medicine, myths, history, religious texts, and astrology. Calendrical information is also included in the books, such as the following fragment that narrates the creation of the uninal (the Maya month in the 365-day calendar). One excerpt reads, "Thus it was set in order by the first wise man, merchise, the first prophet, Napuctun, sacerdote, the first priest. This is the song of how the creation of the uinal [sic] came to pass when the world was not yet created. Then he began to march by his own force. And then said his mother's mother, then said his mother's sister, then said his father's mother [or mother's grandmother], then said his sister-in-law, 'How shall we make manifest and see man upon the road?' These were their words while they marched, but there was no man then. Then they arrived there in the east and began to speak: 'Who has passed here? Here are footsteps; measure it off with your feet.' These were the words of the mistress of the world. Then our Lord, Dios supreme, measured it off with his feet. This is what he first said: ''The count is twelve paces, twelve paces.' This was set in order by Oxlahun Oc. His feet came up even with one another. They departed from the east and spoke its name when the day had no name. He marched on with his mother's mother, with his mother's sister, with his father's mother and with his sister-in-law. The uinal was created; the day was created; that was its name. Sky and earth, ebb water, land rocks and trees were created. The things of sea and land were created."[38]

Mayan astronomy is a complex subject that requires knowledge of arithmetic and acute observation skills. The Maya believed the gods expressed their will through the movements of the stars, so observing and recording their movements were regarded as highly essential activities. Evidence of this complex development can be found in pottery, mural paintings, stone monuments, and codices.

To develop deep knowledge of planetary and star cycles, the Maya required places where they could carry out detailed observations of the sky. Thus, many important cities had observatories, carefully placed in strategic locations allowing Mayan astronomers to have clear views of the celestial realm. Continuous observation of the Sun allowed them to find precise dates for important events such as equinoxes and solstices. In many places, buildings were aligned with these astronomical phenomena. It was also common to align certain buildings with particular celestial bodies. In these cases, the structure contained a specific point from which the star or planet could be clearly observed, such as a doorway, a window, or an altar.

---

[38] Excerpt from the Chilam Balam narrating the creation of the uinal (Roys, 1920, p. 363).

The ancient Mesoamericans did not use tools such as telescopes to aid their observations of the skies, so the Maya managed to develop such an accurate calendar system using only their eyes. To trace the cycle of the Sun, for example, they watched it from a fixed location for several years and recorded its position during the different seasons. In conjunction with that, noteworthy events such as the solstices and equinoxes became important time markers since they could be easily identified year after year.

Spanish chroniclers noted the relevance the Sun had for the ancient Maya and made notes of this in their documents, such as this fragment written by Jacinto de la Serna in 1656: "From one summer to another summer, or better to say from one spring to the other, according to the annual revolution of the Sun observed by all these barbarian nations, by nobles and commoners, peasants and sages[,] regarding the agriculture, our natural summer begins in February because, at this time, the southern winds start blowing and the earth begins to warm up and the trees start flowering in this new Spain."[39]

While the Sun was certainly the most observed celestial body, the Moon and Venus were also the focus of detailed observations, and their cycles were used to mark important ceremonial events. Some historians[40] believe that some

---

[39] Jacinto de la Serna 1953 [1656], chap. VII, 2, cited in Šprajc and Sanchez Nava (2016, p. 202).
[40] See Thompson (1974, p. 91).

pages found in codices even record the cycles of other planets, such as Jupiter, Mars, Mercury, and Saturn.

Venus is one of the most relevant celestial elements in ancient Mayan cosmology, and its different observable positions led the Maya to give it different names, such as: *noh ek* (the great star), *chac ek* (the red star), *sastal ek* (the bright star), *ah-sahcab* (the guide or companion of the aurora), and *xux ek* (the bee or wasp star).[41] *The Dresden Codex* contains a Venus almanac, and representations of the planet frequently appear in many forms on monuments, buildings, murals, and pottery.

Spanish chronicler Diego de Landa was the first one to mention the role Venus played in Mayan astronomy and religion. Other chroniclers like Herrera and Sahagun, as well as colonial manuscripts, mention Venus in relation to the morning star, and some even speak of a relationship between Venus and the god Quetzalcoatl.

It is unclear whether the Maya recorded the cycles of Mercury, but there is evidence in the *Chilam Balam* associating Mercury with illness, robbery, death, and drunkenness. In the *Popol Vuh*, Mercury is represented as an owl and appears related to the underworld. Two different aspects of the planet are shown, Macaw Owl and Shooting Owl, with the former being identified as the messenger of

---

[41] Tozzer, 1941, p. 155

Xibalba. In the codices, Mercury is associated with Chac and Kukulcan and also appears as an owl.

Mars was also an important planet observed by the Maya. *The Dresden Codex* contains a Mars table wherein a 780-day cycle is recorded, as well as an almanac that indicates a 78-day retrograde period. Mars beasts have been identified in *The Dresden Codex* and appear as snouted beasts with cleft hooves, stylized horns, and a stippled underbody in some cases. The beast has been identified as a deer.

In the case of other planets available for observation by the Maya, the Katun cycle was probably used to track the movements of Jupiter and Saturn. Synodic intervals of both planets have been recorded on several monuments in sites like Palenque, Tikal, Copan, and Yaxchilan.

Monkeys played an important role in Mayan astronomical narratives. In some accounts, spider monkeys represented the Sun, and in others, they represented the Sun's younger brother who transformed into Venus, Mars, or Jupiter. In the *Popol Vuh*, the jealous older brothers of the Hero Twins are also transformed into monkeys, only in this case they have been identified as howler monkeys and believed to represent Mars. In addition, spider monkeys seem to be associated with sunset imagery, while howler monkeys were associated with the dawn.

Research suggests that "some war events may relate to

planetary conjunctions."[42] In military planning, the cycle of Venus was used to determine the most auspicious times for going to war. Evidence of this is found in codices and even mural paintings.[43]

It is difficult to identify planetary gods with certainty, but their astronomical characters can be inferred from certain graphic elements. An assembly of astronomical gods is depicted on a bench in Copan; Venus, the Sun, the Moon, and Mars are evident. Also in Copan, a building—known as Structure 22—has a scene representing seven astronomical deities on the Cosmic Monster's back with cloud symbols. Similar scenes are present at Quirigua's Monument 16, Palenque's Temple of the Sun, and Tikal's Stela 31. Additional buildings at Palenque also contain representations of several astronomical gods, many of which are portrayed as deities with animal features. The evidence clearly shows that scenes depicting assemblies of astronomical gods were important themes, and they are represented on different media. Several of these scenes show sets of seven gods, possibly a reference to the seven planets of classical antiquity.

Not only did the Maya observe and record the Sun, Moon, and planets, but there is also evidence indicating that temporary celestial phenomena such as comets, meteors,

---

[42] Milbrath, 1999, p. 242

[43] The Dresden and Cospi codices show representations of Venus related to characters armed with lances. Similar associations are evident in the Bonampak murals.

supernovas, stars, constellations, and even the Milky Way were important to them. These elements were of lesser importance and are represented as accessories or companions instead of gods, but some of the metaphorical images used to portray them are flowers, fireflies, and jaguar spots.

Among these astronomical elements, constellations seem to have had the greatest importance for the Maya. The Pleiades are represented as a rattlesnake's rattle, Orion's Belt as a turtle, Scorpius as a scorpion, and Sagittarius as a fish-snake combination. The Milky Way is represented as a Cosmic Monster, a celestial river, or a sky serpent. Stars are described in the *Chilam Balam* as "flowers of the night," and the night sky is referred to as the "flowering sky." In *The Madrid Codex*, stars are described as "eyes of the night." In addition, individual stars may be represented by certain birds.

The Mayan Worldview

As is true of every society, the Maya had their own unique way of conceiving the world and their place within it. In the Mayan worldview, the earth was divided into four sections or directions, which were clearly based on observations of the Sun's yearly cycle and the knowledge of the equinoxes and solstices. East and west were sacred points since, as mentioned above, they corresponded to the directions in which the Sun rose and set. North and south were also meaningful since they were associated with the solstices. The importance of these four points is evidenced in the glyphs found that represent each one. Each direction has a set of symbols: a color, a *ceiba*[44] tree on which a bird is perched, a type of corn, a type of beans, and a series of animals. The trees hold up the sky alongside four anthropomorphic deities called *bacabes* or *pahuahtunes,* whose role was to organize the world. The colors correspond to the type of corn included in each section: white for north, black for west, yellow for south, and red for east. This fourfold concept did not only apply to the earth, but was also present in the celestial realm and the underworld. Mark explained, "There were four deities in particular, known as The Bearers of the Years [the Bacab] who held the four cardinal points of the sky and imbued a particular year with certain energy. Muluc was the Bacab of the east and his years were always positive in energy. He was associated with the color red. Kan was the Bacab of the south, associated with yellow, and also brought good fortune. Ix, the Bacab of the north was linked with the color white while Cauac, The Bacab of the west's color was black and both of them brought negative energy and bad fortune to the year."[45]

The Mayan universe was geocentric, and they believed that

---

[44] The ceiba is a type of tree native to tropical regions in North and South America and Africa, also known as kapok or silk-cotton tree. It had a very importance significance for the Maya.

[45] Mark, 2012

celestial heroes traveled across the realms from the sky to the earth to the underworld and vice versa.

One of the greatest misunderstandings or interpretations about the ancient Maya is the belief that they predicted the end of the world. There is no archaeological or historical evidence to support this claim; in fact, rather than believing in "endings," the Maya believed in the idea of repeating cycles. This is quite evident in their complex calendar system. The Mayan concept of time was not only linear but cyclical, and their gods lived on this plane. The gods existed much like humans - they were born, developed, sustained themselves, carried out their specific roles, and died, but then they were reborn. The Maya's entire temporal system followed this pattern.

Mayan kings were thought to be of divine origin, and Prudence Rice has suggested that the "foundation of Maya[n] kings' power and divinity was esoteric knowledge about time."[46] The relationship between Mayan rulers and time has been established by many researchers, and terms like "rulers of time," "embodiments of time and its passage," and "those whose dynasties owed their mandates to the control of time" have been used by scholars to mark this connection.[47] The manipulation of time creates the illusion of having control over it and is therefore a useful tool for

---

[46] Rice, 2008, p. 275
[47] Rice, 2008, p. 275

establishing social and cosmic order. In this sense, time is a key aspect of "cosmo-political power".[48] Time did not only represent cosmic order, but also supplied a kind of cosmic sanction to ensure social order and political power.

The Mayan word for king is *ajaw,* and it was often preceded by the term *k'inich,* which means "sun-faced." This established a clear connection between the figure of the ruler and the Sun. For Mayan rulers, "a carefully crafted illusion of 'control' of time constituted the armature of an ideology of the sacred king as an embodiment of the Sun, and that powerful and precise calendars and time itself were politico-ritually deployed and manipulated as instruments of power by the ruling dynasties."[49]

Mayan kings used ritual power in conjunction with astronomical observations and their calendar system as a means of displaying their divinity and asserting their authority. The use of this powerful combination of elements allowed the kings to experience a transformation in which they became incarnations of gods. This process of transformation has been recorded on monumental inscriptions, which consist of a series of dates following the calendrical system and a text with the dedication of the monument. This narrative typically presents a list of similarities between the life of the king and the life of a god,

---

[48] Munn (1992) cited in Rice (2008, p. 290).
[49] Rice, 2008, p. 276

and in that way it establishes a connection between them:
"When ancient Maya…linked the mythical deeds of their
gods and the lives of their rulers through complex
calendrical associations, or spoke about the reoccurrence of
calendrical configurations in the future, it has been
interpreted in terms of mythical exemplarity or as an
apology of power…rulers were not powerful because they
represented things, they were powerful themselves, masters
of ritual relationships, of ontological transformations. Art
did not justify their power[;] it created their power."[50]

When a king dedicated a monument, the accompanying
inscription immortalized him for posterity, leaving a
permanent link between him and the god with whom he was
now associated. This placed his actions within the sphere of
cyclical time as he would be reborn with each new cycle,
just like the god he embodied.

Archaeoastronomical[51] studies have been conducted on
many Mayan sites and have concluded that many important
structures were oriented in accordance with astronomical
events and their calendrical system. Sunrises and sunsets on
specific days of the year seemed to be one of the most
commonly used elements with which to orient buildings.[52]
These architectural alignments "exemplify the significance
of astronomical and calendrical factors in the concepts

---

[50] Zamora, 2016, p. 79

[51] Archaeoastronomy is a branch of archaeology that focuses on the study of astronomy in ancient cultures.

[52] "Tikal Mayan Ruins," 2017

dictating architectural design and urban planning."[53] The buildings' orientations served as observational calendars, allowing the Maya to plan and schedule a variety of rituals and activities throughout the year.

Some ceremonies carried out in these settings were solar rituals. In these cases, buildings with specific alignment to certain solar phenomena became the stage for these events. The solar phenomena identified as being important in architectural orientation are zenith passages, solstices, and equinoxes. Alignments related to the Sun were based on observational calendars destined to facilitate the programming of agricultural activities and their associated rituals during the yearly cycle. An east-west alignment seems of particular importance due to its undisputable relationship to the rising and setting of the Sun.

These alignments are found at important sites like Uaxactun, Calakmul, Tikal, Dzibilchaltun, Uxmal, and Palenque, but perhaps the best-known example is in the Castillo at Chichen Itza. On the equinoxes, the shadows create the form of a serpent on the north (at sunset) and south (at dawn) sides of the structure. "The astronomical alignments cannot be adequately understood only in terms of their practical function…they are incorporated in important civic and ceremonial buildings, revealing that the utilitarian function of astronomy was embedded in ritual and intimately

---

[53] Šprajc, Morales-Aguilar, and Hansen, 2009, p. 79

related with social life, religion, and political affairs of Pre-Hispanic societies."[54]

A photo of the serpent effect at the Castillo during the spring equinox in 2009

[54] Šprajc, Morales-Aguilar, and Hansen, 2009, p. 95

**Bjørn Christian Tørrissen's picture of the serpent effect
at night using artificial light**

Several types of buildings could be aligned to specific astronomical events, the most common being temples, administrative buildings, and palaces. It is interesting to note that there does not seem to be any kind of correlation between the types of buildings and specific alignment, so structures oriented with solstices were not of a specific type. "Astronomical alignments in specialized buildings can offer a sense of the way architectural space was arranged opportunistically to accommodate timed rituals."[55]

The Maya were not the only ancient people to orient buildings according to solstices, and there are many examples of this practice in ancient history. Sanchez Nava and Šprajc wrote, "Since the solstices, marked by the extremes of the Sun's trajectory along the horizon, are naturally significant moments of the tropical year, they must have been the most elementary references for orientation in time and the seasonal cycle. Furthermore, being apparently critical moments, when the [s]un changes the course of its annual movement, the solstices acquired great symbolic significance and inspired a variety of ritual practices."[56]

The orientation of buildings also corresponded to four important moments in the agricultural calendar. In the maize cycle, land plots were prepared in February, and the rain season, beginning in May, was when planting was done. After that, the first maize cobs ripened in August, and October and November marked the harvest season.

A set of architectural alignments found on many Mayan sites, known as E-group assemblages, seem to be further evidence of the importance of astronomy in building orientation. These clusters have a structure located to the west, and three structures on the opposite side were placed on a north-south axis. Archaeologist Frans Blom[57] first discovered this alignment in 1924 at Uaxactun in Guatemala

---

[55] Aveni et al., 2003, p. 159
[56] Sanchez Nava and Šprajc, 2016, p. 201
[57] See Aimers and Rice (2006).

and noticed that the three buildings on the north-south axis were set to mark the sunrise during equinoxes and solstices when viewed from the structure on the west. Blom proposed that these E-groups functioned as solar observatories, but later studies[58] have suggested their function might have been ritualistic instead, including ceremonies like agricultural rituals. According to Aveni, "E-group complexes served, at least at some time in the course of their development, as devices intended for marking time according to a zenith Sun-based seasonal calendar. [These] complexes may have served as social focal points, their open spaces perhaps intended for ritual displays by an emerging theocratic elite."[59]

According to Anthony Aveni, Anne Dowd, and Benjamin Vining,[60] "if seeing the Sun can be shown to have been part of the [architectural] scheme, then regardless of whether the Maya were watching it scientifically or ceremonially, the associated architectural complex may be regarded as an observatory." They believe that, before the Maya developed a written calendar, they used architectural alignments, "orientation calendars," among which the E-group complex at Uaxactun is the earliest example and could have been used to mark important moments in the annual calendar.

Archaeoastronomical research has also revealed that some architectural elements were aligned to the extremes of the

---

[58] Aimers and Rice, 2006
[59] Aveni, et al., 2003, pp. 171-172
[60] Aveni, et al., 2003, p. 172

Moon and Venus. Despite the complications associated with tracking their movements, the Maya clearly had records of their synodic cycles, moments during the year when they were visible (particularly in the case of Venus), and eclipses (in the case of the Moon). The influence of Venus in architecture is clearly seen at Uxmal in Yucatan, Mexico, where the "House of the Governor" bears a façade full of Venus symbols, and the building itself seems to have been constructed to allow observations of Venus. From the central doorway, an alignment of the planet with other monuments on the site is present, marking its movement throughout the year.

"Venus orbits the Sun approximately every 225 days," but from Earth, it appears to move back and forth in a cycle that lasts 584 days[61]. For Mayan astronomers and priests, it seemed significant that five of these Venus cycles corresponded to eight solar years. In addition, Venus has four observable phases. For 250 days, it follows the setting Sun and is referred to as the "Evening Star," before disappearing for eight days and reappearing as the "Morning Star," which corresponds to the 236 days when it is visible before dawn. After that, it disappears again for 90 days, and then the cycle begins once more.[62]

As Sanchez Nava and Šprajc astutely observed, "the

---

[61] Zorich, 2013
[62] Zorich, 2012, p. 28

characteristics of architectural alignments and spatial ordering in Maya[n] cities reflect the complexity of the underlying concepts, in which the astronomically derived ideas were intertwined with beliefs about the natural environment and the structure and functioning of the universe as a whole. The celestial referents of orientations were Venus extremes on the western horizon, the standstill positions of the Moon [sic] and, in most cases, the sunrises and sunsets on specific dates."[63]

One fundamental aspect of the Maya's worldview was their mythology. The stories narrating heroic acts of gods provide ample information allowing us to better understand the relationship they had with cosmic time. A recurring theme in these tales is regeneration and transformation.

The *Popol Vuh* narrates the story of Mayan creation through the tales of hero twins, Hunajpu and Xbalanque, and it was described by one article in detail: "This is an account of the beginning, when all was stillness, silence, and water. There was no light, no land, no plants, no people, and no animals. Six deities, covered…in green and blue feathers, lay in the primordial waters: the Framer and the Shaper, Tepew and Quetzal Serpent, along with Xpiyacóc and Xmucané. These deities, helped Heart of Sky, also known as Hurakán, create the Earth. Their spirit essence and their miraculous power gave the Earth its creative energy. Now

---

[63] Sanchez Nava and Šprajc, 2016, pp. 208-209

the land had a heart, and they called it Heart of Earth. To separate the sky from the Earth they planted a tall ceiba tree, making space for all life. The roots penetrated deep into the nine levels of the Maya Underworld, the trunk was on the surface of the land, and the branches reached up to the thirteen levels of the Maya Upper-world. The plants were next created to live on the Earth. And then the animals were created. But the animals did not speak and could not worship. So the deities decided to create human beings from mud. But these first humans had no souls and were not good 'keepers of the days.' They destroyed them in a great flood. The deities tried another time, and created humans from wood. But the wooden people could not worship either, so they were destroyed. Those that survived are said to have become the monkeys in the trees. The sky and Earth now existed, but there was no Sun [sic] and no Moon. A vain bird called Seven Macaw claimed to be the Sun and the Moon. But this was not true. Two amazing Twins [sic], Hunajpu and Xbalanqué, defeated Seven Macaw, by shooting him with darts. The Hero Twins were conceived, when their mother, Ixkik', spoke to the decapitated…head of their father, Hun Hunahpu, who spit on her hand from a cacao tree. Hun Hunahpu had been killed by the Lords of Xibalbá, the Underworld. The Hero Twins became great ball players, and to bring their Father [sic] back to life, they challenged the Lords of the Underworld to a game in Xibalbá. The twins were permitted to play the ball game only after they had survived the dangerous trials set for them in the Underworld. Using great skill and cunning, the twins won the ball game, and this allowed their slain father to come back to life as the Maize God. The Hero Twins left Xibalbá and climbed back up to the surface of the Earth. They continued up into the sky, becoming the Sun, and the Moon. Now that the Sun and Moon were in the sky and illuminated the Earth, the deities created the final form of human beings using white and yellow corn. Corn is the precious substance that ultimately succeeds in producing true, and enduring, humans."[64]

Another tale, the myth of the Xtabay, tells the story of Xkeban, the sinner, and Utz-Colel, the virtuous, who go through a transformation in death. J.J. Mark explained, "Xkeban, though considered a sinner for having sex outside of marriage, was more virtuous than the self-righteous and cold Utz-Colel and, when she died, filled the village with sweet perfume and exotic wildflowers known as Xtabentun grew on her grave. Nothing grew on the grave of Utz-Colel but she was transformed into the cactus without scent, the Tzacam, and the flower known as the Xtabay who also appears as a kind of succubus who waylays unsuspecting traveling men, seduces them, and destroys them."[65]

Another tale of transformation is the legend of the

[64] "The Creation Story of the Maya," 2021
[65] Mark, 2012

Maquech, which narrates the story of a princess named
Cuzan who falls in love with a man her father does not deem
worthy of her. The princess enlists the help of a shaman,
who turns her lover into an insect so that she can keep him
with her forever. A similar account, the tale of Nicte Ha,
also highlights the concept of transformation. The legend is
about a pair of lovers who, in order to be together, are
transformed into a red bird and a divine lotus that dwell
along the banks of a sacred cenote for all eternity.

For the ancient Maya, there was a strong connection
between astronomy and astrology since their scientific
observations of the stars and planets had religious and
esoteric functions in many cases and were used for
divination, predictions, and prophecy.Many studies have
focused on trying to interpret glyphs found in codices,
particularly *The Paris Codex* and other pictographic
representations as constellations.[66] This has led many to
believe in the existence of a Mayan zodiac, and certain
correspondences between Mayan representations and our
current zodiac have further supported this notion. The best
example of a zodiac is found in *The Paris Codex*, where 13
animal signs have been identified and linked to
constellations. The glyphs show a rattlesnake, scorpion, bat,
turtle, frog, and two birds, and the rest of the animals seem
to be fantastic beasts. The table in the codex "shows five

---

[66] See Villela and Schele (1996).

rows of *Tzolkin* dates with red numerals spaced at intervals
of 28 days," which should be read from right to left. In the
top row, "between each zodiac figure, black numbers record
intervals of 8.8 in Long Round notation [168 days],
representing six 'months.' Alongside the intervals of 168
days, blue-green numbers record correction factors that
serve to realign the *Tzolkin* calendar dates with the solar year
and the position of the constellations."[67]

The façade of the Nunnery or Las Monjas at Chichen Itza
shows what some researchers have identified as another type
of zodiac. It contains a series of animals and a lunar glyph.
The elements on the façade only have a slight overlap with
those of *The Paris Codex*. Yet another building, the Palace
of the Stuccoes at Acanceh in Yucatan, also presents a
sequence of 21 animals thought by some to be a zodiac. A
frog, a bat, a feline, a gopher, an owl, and a rattlesnake are
some of the animals identified. A few of them correspond to
those in *The Paris Codex*. Those who support the idea of this
being a zodiac believe the 21 figures represent the 13
constellations, and the remaining five correspond to the Sun,
Moon, Venus, and possibly another two planets. Despite
these examples, there are still those who doubt that any of
the glyphs actually correspond to a zodiac, and it is possible
that historians will never know for sure.[68]

---

[67] Milbrath, 1999, p. 254
[68] Milbrath, 1999, p. 10

For the ancient Maya, the cycles of Venus and other events like eclipses had both astronomical and astrological functions. For example, Venus was a force to be feared. In some illustrations in *The Dresden Codex*, Venus gods are shown throwing spears and launching dire warnings. In a similar nature, solar eclipses were considered "occasions of dire peril,"[69] and the Maya believed they were associated with the end of the world. The Maya, therefore, tried to predict these events so they might have time to prevent them from happening altogether with rituals and ceremonies. The lunar table in *The Dresden Codex* was thus used as a prediction tool and had a prophetic function. The codex also contains glyphs that have been interpreted as constellations.

For the Maya, "each day had favorable or unfavorable auguries, determined only by trained specialists for various activities depending on the confluence of cosmic forces governing their destinies."[70] These special priests or sorcerers were in charge of carrying out specific ceremonies to read the almanacs and make prognostications about the following cycle. Diego de Landa described one such ritual in a passage of his book, *Relacion de las cosas de Yucatan:* "During the month Uo the priests, the physicians and sorcerers, who are all the same thing, began to prepare by fasts and other things for the celebration of another festival. The hunters and fishers solemnized it on the seventh day [of

---

[69] Thompson, 1974, p. 88
[70] Rice, 2008, p. 282

the month] Zip, and each of them celebrated it for himself on his own day. First the priests celebrated theirs, which they called Pocam. Having assembled, clothed in their ornaments, at the house of the lord, first they drove away the evil spirit as usual; then they took out their books and spread them out on the fresh boughs which they had for this purpose, and invoking with prayers and devotions and idol named Kinich Ahau Itzamna, who they say was the first priest, they offered him gifts and presents and burned before him their balls of incense with the new fire. Meanwhile they dissolved in a vessel a little of their verdigris with virgin water, which they said had been brought from the woods where a woman had never penetrated. With this they anointed the boards of their books so as to purify them. This having been done, the most learned of the priests opened a book and looked at the prognostics of that year."[71]

As mentioned above, the books of *Chilam Balam* contain texts on a variety of subjects, including astrological information, and several pages are dedicated to zodiacs and horoscopes. Zodiacal houses are assigned to each month, and each sign on the horoscope is accompanied by prognostications for blood purging. The seven days of the week are named according to the seven planets used in European astrology.

The *Chilam Balam* uses the *Tzolkin* to cast predictions on a

---

[71] Tozzer, 1941, pp. 153-154

person's destiny upon birth. The 20 named days are Imix, Ik, Akbal, Kan, Chicchan, Cimi, Manik, Lamat, Muluc, Oc, Chuen, Eb, Ben Ix, Men, Cib, Caban, Edznab, Cauac, and Ahau. The day on which a child was born determined their fate - for example, if a person was born on 1 Kan, they were believed to be Ah Itznam, or wise, the nightingale was their bird, and their tree was the red ceiba. The color red was associated with the east. This day was considered greatly auspicious, and those born on it would likely have abundance, wealth, and happiness.

In addition to predicting a person's fate, the *Tzolkin* also indicated which days were most favorable for a variety of things, such as having ceremonies, administering medicine, hunting, and carrying out agricultural activities. These predictions were a fundamental part of daily life for the Maya since they guided their everyday activities.

Religious rituals carried out by the Maya could take place at regular intervals, meaning they were repeated periodically or were occasionally enacted when the situation required it. Cyclical rituals were thought to keep the balance between life and death, organized according to the *Haab* or 365-day calendar. This was also called the religious year because each period of 20 days had a main god for whom different ceremonies were held.

Some of the most important rituals celebrated according to

the Mayan calendar were those taking place during the *Wayeb*, the short month of only five days, occurring at the end of the *Haab*. De Orellana explained, "This time span was a problematic one indeed since it was not part of the regular cycles and responded to the belief that time–just like the universe, human beings or nature–grew old, wore out and was headed towards [sic] death; however, just as the vegetation would grow green again year after year and social life was renewed, time also initiated a new cycle."[72]

Ritual activities increased during the *Wayeb*, and these days were considered chaotic and uncertain, associated with darkness and the possible death of the Sun. Due to this, the most solemn celebrations took place during these five days. It was considered a favorable time for the ancestors to visit Earth and was charged with symbolic elements. People feared misfortune, and therefore they only left their homes to participate in religious ceremonies. Many purification rituals were carried out in the hope of warding off bad luck for the following year.

Lars Pharo identified a new concept called "ritual practice of time," which "represents a ceremonial completion, a period-ending, and an introduction of a given period of time in calendars. These time-intervals, time-endings and inaugurations of new time periods are observed in ritual practices."[73] These rituals of time were public events in

---

[72] De Orellana et al., 2012, p. 93

which the entire community could take part. In the case of the Maya, these time rituals were linked to the *Tzolkin*.

The Maya "recorded the mythical actions of their deities, which cyclically [like astronomical phenomena] or capriciously [like human moods] shaped events in the universe."[74] One of their oldest beliefs was that of the cyclical destruction of the universe, an event that led to the birth of a new era. Period-ending rituals had the objective of recreating the world and renewing time. There were also ceremonies held at the beginning of the new year. Itzamna, the celestial creator, was one of the gods worshipped during this time.

The following fragment from Diego de Landa provides details about the new year rituals: "The first day of Pop, which is the first month of the Indians, was their new year and was a very solemn festival among them; as it was universal and all took part in it and so the whole town jointly made the feast to all the idols. To celebrate it with more solemnity, they renewed on this day all the objects which they made use of, such as plates, vessels, stools, mats and old clothes and the stuffs [sic] with which they wrapped up their idols."[75]

The *Tzolkin* was widely used as a divinatory calendar and

---

[73] Pharo, 2009, p. 15
[74] De Orellana et al., 2012, p. 95
[75] Tozzer, 1941, p. 151

was used to determine the fate and name of newborns. It was also believed that a child's date of birth on the 260-day calendar would influence their character, behavior, identity, and destiny. One of the rituals intimately linked to the *Tzolkin* was the Burner Ceremonies, held every 65 days. This allowed for four of these ceremonies in each 260-day cycle. Burner periods were recorded in divination almanacs, marking fortunate days in which the ceremonies could be held. Fire ceremonies were among the most important parts of the rituals. Each period of 65 days was further subdivided into three intervals of 20 days and one interval of five days. These four intervals began on four specific days - Chicchan, Oc, Men, and Ahau - and represented the cardinal directions and had a color associated with each one. Chicchan corresponded to the east and red, Oc to the north and white, Men to the west and black, and Ahau to the south and yellow. In *The Dresden Codex*, Chac[76] appears as the main character in these ceremonies. Time and space were symbolically juxtaposed in the rituals and followed a continuum on a 260-day cycle that would then start over and begin a new cycle.

The historical information collected by the Spanish during colonial times offers a great compilation of the large variety of cyclical rituals carried out by the Maya. According to Landa, there were specific ceremonies taking place during

---

[76] Chac is the Mayan god of rain, the equivalent of Tlaloc in central Mexico.

each month of their solar calendar: "In the month of Zotz, the owners of hives of honey prepared to celebrate their festival in Tzec; and although the principal preparation for these festivals was fasting, it was only obligatory 'on the priest and the officers who assisted him,' and it was voluntary for the others."[77] Tozzer elaborated on this, writing, "On a day of this month Zac, which the priest designated, the hunters celebrated another festival like that which they had celebrated in the month Zip. They celebrated this one now to appease the gods and to turn aside the anger which they would have against them and their sowings. They made [these feasts] on account of the blood which they had spilled during their hunts; for they considered as an abomination any bloodshed unless it was in their sacrifices. And on this account whenever they went hunting, they invoked the god and burned their incense to him, and, if they could, they anointed his face with the blood of the heart of whatever game they had killed."[78]

To this day, the descendants of the Maya still use ancient astronomical knowledge that has been passed down through the generations. One area of their lives in which this is most evident is the agricultural cycle. The observation of the Sun and phenomena such as the spring equinox and the position of the Milky Way still give them the information they rely upon year after year.

---

[77] de Landa, 1937
[78] Tozzer, 1941, pp. 156, 162

The following words, narrated by a modern Maya, clearly expresses the way old traditions permeate the contemporary worldview: "In our Maya tradition, time is cyclical, and we believe that all things in the Universe are interconnected. Watching the sky makes it possible for our people to define predictable cycles in our lives…With the arrival of the March equinox, when the day and night are of equal length, the soil is prepared for planting. This is the time when Kukulkán, the feathered serpent, slithers down the pyramid of El Castillo in Chichén Itzá. Our grandparents tell us that Kukulkán is the cord that connects the Earth and the sky…A few months after the equinox, when the Sun [sic] is passing overhead through the center of the sky, we begin planting corn, beans, and squash. This time, called the zenith passage of the Sun, typically coincides with the first rain storms…Late July marks the time of the canícula, a short dry spell when we bend down all the corn stalks before the possibility of a late rainfall. Farmers know when to do this by observing the Milky Way high in the sky and the bright star Sirius rising in the East before sunrise. Our culture remains strong because the Maya way of life is rooted in our communities, our native languages, and a deep understanding of our connection between the Earth and sky."[79]

Meanwhile, research about Mayan astronomy continues, and further studies continue to help researchers unlock

---

[79] "The Maya," 2021

certain secrets of the past. Still, there is plenty left to be discovered. As Susan Milbrath put it, researchers "are only beginning to understand the role of astronomy in Maya imagery. Through iconographic studies focusing on astronomy, decipherment of Maya hieroglyphs, and study of traditions preserved by the Maya today, it may be possible to recognize a wealth of seasonal images and rituals dating back to the Classic Maya period."[80]

Future studies will surely shed light on some of the aspects that remain unknown and contribute to a greater comprehension and appreciation of one of history's most fascinating civilizations.

Online Resources

Other Mesoamerican titles by Charles River Editors

Other titles about Mayan astronomy on Amazon

Further Reading

Aimers, J. J. and P. M. Rice. Astronomy, Ritual, and the Interpretation of Maya 'E-Group' Architectural Assemblages. *Ancient Mesoamerica*, vol. 17, no. 1, pp. 79–96.

Aveni, A. F., et al. (2003). Maya Calendar Reform? Evidence from Orientations of Specialized Architectural

---

[80] Milbrath, 1999, p. 292

Assemblages. *Latin American Antiquity*, vol. 14, no. 2, pp. 159–178.

Baaijens, T. (1995). The Typical "Landa Year" as the First Step in the Correlation of the Maya and the Christian Calendar. *Mexicon*, vol. 17, no. 3, pp. 50-51.

Barrera, L. (2012). Concepción Del Tiempo y Calendarios En El Chilam Balam De IXIL. *Artes De México*, no. 107, pp. 26–33.

Casares Contreras, O. J. (2016). *Astronomia en el area Maya*. Universidad Autonoma de Yucatan, Merida.

De la Garza C. M. (2010). El universo temporal en el pensamiento Maya. *Arqueología Mexicana*, núm. 103, pp. 38-44.

de Landa, Diego. (1937). Yucatan Before and After the Conquest. *Sacred Texts*, William Gates (Trans.), https://www.sacred-texts.com/nam/maya/ybac/ybac44.htm.

De Orellana, M., et al. (2012). The Art of Maya Timekeeping. *Artes De México*, no. 107, pp. 81-104.

Farriss, N. M. (1987). Remembering the Future, Anticipating the Past: History, Time, and Cosmology among the Maya of Yucatan. *Comparative Studies in Society and History*, vol. 29, no. 3, pp. 566-593.

Hocken, Vigdis and Aparna Kher. (2021). Shortest Day of

the Year in the Northern Hemisphere. *Time and Date*, https://www.timeanddate.com/calendar/december-solstice.html.

Iwaniszewski, S. (2012). Los ciclos lunares y el calendario Maya. *Arqueología Mexicana núm*, 118, pp. 38-42.

Linden, J. H. (1986). Glyph X of the Maya Lunar Series: An Eighteen-Month Lunar Synodic Calendar. *American Antiquity*, vol. 51, no. 1, pp. 122–136.

Makemson, M. W. (1947). The Maya Calendar. *Publications of the Astronomical Society of the Pacific*, vol. 59, no. 346, pp. 17–26.

Mark, J. J. (2012). The Maya Calendar and the End of the World: Why the one does not substantiate the other. *World History Encyclopedia. World History Encyclopedia* https://www.worldhistory.org/article/416/the-maya-calendar-and-the-end-of-the-world-why-the/#citation_info

Metcalfe, Tom. (2020). Mayans built massive structures thousands of years ago. Researchers found the biggest one yet. *Yahoo! News*. https://news.yahoo.com/mayans-built-massive-structures-thousands-190205277.html

Milbrath, S. (1999). *Star Gods of the Maya. Astronomy in Art, Folklore, and Calendars*. University of Texas Press.

Milbrath, S. (2017). The Role of Solar Observations in

Developing The Preclassic Maya Calendar. *Latin American Antiquity*, vol. 28, no. 1, pp. 88–104.

Miller, J. H. (1992). The Princeton Codex of the Book of Chilam Balam of Nah. *The Princeton University Library Chronicle*, vol. 53, no. 3, pp. 287–296.

Pharo, L. K. (2009). The Ritual Practice of Time of the Yucatec Maya 260-Day Calendar in the Post-Classic Period: The Burner Ceremonies of Quadripartite 65-Day Intervals. *Journal of Ritual Studies*, vol. 23, no. 1, pp. 15–27.

Rice, P. M. (2008). Time, Power, and the Maya. *Latin American Antiquity*, vol. 19, no. 3, pp. 275-298.

Roys, R. L. (1920). A Maya Account of the Creation. *American Anthropologist*, vol. 22, no. 4, pp. 360–366.

Sánchez Nava, P. and I. Šprajc. (2012). Orientaciones en la arquitectura maya. Astronomía, calendario y agricultura. *Arqueología Mexicana* núm. 118, pp. 46-55.

Šprajc, I., C. Morales-Aguilar, and R. Hansen. (2009). Early Maya Astronomy and Urban Planning at El Mirador, Peten, Guatemala. *Anthropological Notebooks*, pp. 79-101.

Šprajc, I. and P. Sanchez Nava. (2016). Astronomy and Architecture in the Maya Lowlands. *Journal of Skyscape*

Archaeology, 2, pp. 189-215. DOI. 10.1558/jsa.30050.

The Creation Story of the Maya. (2021). *Smithsonian National Museum of the American Indian.* https://maya.nmai.si.edu/sites/default/files/transcripts/the_cr eation_story_of_the_maya.pdf.

The Dresden Codex. (2017). *World Digital Library*. https://www.wdl.org/en/item/11621/.

The Maya: Connecting the Earth and Sky. (2021). *Smithsonian National Museum of the American Indian.* https://maya.nmai.si.edu/sites/default/files/transcripts/connec ting_earth_and_sky.pdf.

The Mayan Prediction. (2012). *Is the World Going to End in 2021?* https://yoyofacts.blogspot.com/.

Thompson, J. E. S. (1974). Maya Astronomy. *Philosophical Transactions of the Royal Society of London. Series A, Mathematical and Physical Sciences*, vol. 276, no. 1257, pp. 83–98.

Tikal Mayan Ruins. (2017). *Travel Blog*, https://www.travelblog.org/Central-America-Caribbean/Guatemala/Peten-Region/Tikal/blog-992905.html.

Tozzer, A. (1941). Landa's Relacion de las Cosas de Yucatan: a Translation. *Papers of the Peabody Museum of*

American Archaeology and Ethnology. Harvard University, Cambridge.

Vail, G. and A. Aveni. (2004). Research Methodologies and New Approaches Into Interpreting the Madrid Codex. In *The Madrid Codex: New Approaches to Understanding and Ancient Maya Manuscript, Chapter 1*, pp. 1-32. https://www.upcolorado.com/excerpts/9780870818615.pdf.

Valencia Rivera, R. (2017). El Tiempo Vuela: El Uso De Aves y Otros Animales Para Representar Las Unidades De Tiempo De La Cuenta Larga Maya. *Journal De La Société Des Américanistes*, vol. 103, pp. 399–428.

Villela, K. and L. Schele. (1993). Astronomy and the Iconography of Creation Among the Classic and Colonial Period Maya. In *Eighth Palenque Round Table*, Merle Greene Robertson, Martha J. Macri, and Jan McHargue (Eds.). Pre-Columbian Art Research Institute.

Zamora, A. (2016). Deciphering Ontologies: Divination and 'Infinition' in Classic Maya Inscriptions. *Revista De Antropologia*, vol. 59, no. 3, pp. 73–89.

Zorich, Z. (2012). The Maya Sense of Time. *Archaeology*, vol. 65, no. 6, pp. 25–29.

Zorich, Z. (2013). An Eye on Venus. *Archaeology*, https://www.archaeology.org/issues/44-1211/features/304-uxmal-venus.

Free Books by Charles River Editors

We have brand new titles available for free most days of the week. To see which of our titles are currently free, click on this link.

Discounted Books by Charles River Editors

We have titles at a discount price of just 99 cents everyday. To see which of our titles are currently 99 cents, click on this link.

www.ingramcontent.com/pod-product-compliance
Lightning Source LLC
Chambersburg PA
CBHW081933120726
47997CB00010B/3132